D0174968

UPGRADED TO SERIOUS

Books by Heather McHugh

POEMS

Upgraded to Serious

Eyeshot

The Father of the Predicaments

Hinge & Sign: Poems, 1968–1993

Shades

To the Quick

A World of Difference

Dangers

PROSE

Broken English: Poetry and Partiality

TRANSLATIONS

Cyclops by Euripides

Glottal Stop: 101 Poems by Paul Celan
(with Nikolai Popov)

Because the Sea Is Black: Poems by Blaga Dimitrova
(with Nikolai Popov)

D'Après Tout: Poems by Jean Follain

ANTHOLOGY

The Best American Poetry 2007
(with David Lehman)

Upgraded to Serious

Heather McHugh

COPPER CANYON PRESS

Port Townsend, Washington

Printed in the United States of America

Cover art: ©iStockphoto.com / Joan Kimball

Copper Canyon Press is in residence at Fort Worden State Park in Port Townsend, Washington, under the auspices of Centrum. Centrum is a gathering place for artists and creative thinkers from around the world, students of all ages and backgrounds, and audiences seeking extraordinary cultural enrichment.

LIBRARY OF CONGRESS CATALOGING-IN-PUBLICATION DATA

McHugh, Heather, 1948-
Upgraded to serious / Heather McHugh.
p. cm.
ISBN 978-1-55659-306-2 (cloth: alk. paper)
I. Title.
PS3563.A311614U64 2009
811′.54–dc22
2009013347

3 5 7 9 8 6 4 2
FIRST PRINTING

COPPER CANYON PRESS
Post Office Box 271
Port Townsend, Washington 98368

www.coppercanyonpress.org

To my mother, who has loved literature all her life, and who turned ninety-one the year I finished this book, I dedicate it.

ACKNOWLEDGMENTS

The American Scholar: "And the Greatest of These," "Boondocks," "Man in the Street" (under the title "Hand over Mouth"), "No Sex for Priests," "Unto High Heaven," "Which Is Given for You" (under the title "A Smattering")

The Best American Poetry 2006 (eds. Paul Muldoon and David Lehman): "Ill-Made Almighty"

Boston Review: "An Underworldliness"

Botanica (a poem portfolio designed by Enid Mark): "The River Overflows the Rift"

Electronic Poetry Review: "Thous by the Thousands"

Fence: "For Want of Better Words"

Ink Node: "On Purpose Laid," "Study Under Fire"

The New Yorker: "Hackers Can Sidejack Cookies"

Poetry: "Dark View," "Half Border and Half Lab," "Myrrha to the Source," "Not to Be Dwelled On," "Philosopher Orders Crispy Pork," "Space Bar"

Poetry London: "Both Sides Snipe at the Holy Ghost," "Nocebo"

Poetry Northwest: "Glass House," "Mary's Reminder"

TriQuarterly: "Far Niente," reprinted in *Writing Poems,* 7th ed. (ed. Michelle Boisseau)

The Washington Post: "Half Border and Half Lab," "Not to Be Dwelled On"

World Poetry: "A Blind" (under the title "A Blind of Green")

A tip of the hat to United States Artists, and to the Creative Writing Program at the University of Washington: they afforded me time in which to write the poems in this book. Merrie-Ellen Wilcox, editor and friend, patiently fielded a flurry of eleventh-hour misgivings. Many of these pieces were written in honor of friends I loved who died during these past few years, leaving rips in the fabric of the world. I wish to acknowledge them here, and bless their having been: Elliot Fishbein, Patty Swanson, Karen Shabetai, and Karen Tepfer.

I use white-black life gain and self-burn, green-black discard rush,
and blue-green buildup creature crush.

OVERHEARD IN CONVERSATION

I love Method, extremely.

CLENARD THE GRAMMARIAN,
IN A DIALOGUE BY MATTHEW PRIOR

CONTENTS

UPGRADED TO SERIOUS

IDENTICAL MULTIPLES

Inside the zygote
something's simmering.
It's boiling up and boiling over

until suddenly a second one
splits off. Now there's a calm
accumulation until one of those two
gets its own upbubbling baby-making urge
and percolates itself into a rift. So that makes three

pursuing their apparently peace-loving
self-abutting industries... And all night long
the dreamer's implicated, doubled over, doubled up
as mixer/muller of the parts – hormonal cauldron where a lot
of mental matter too is stirred. Eventually a being will conceive
(in stalls of staves, in calques of cramp, in knuckleheads and thrall –

god help us all) the stems of words.

FASTENER

One as is as another as.
One with is with another with;

one against's against all others and one of
of all the ofs on earth feels chosen. So the man

can't help his fastening on many
(since the likes of him like

look-alikes)... When the star-shower crosses
the carnival sky, then the blues of the crowd

try to glisten, to match it; and the two
who work late in the butcher-house touch,

reaching just the same moment
for glue and for hatchet.

WEBCAM THE WORLD

Get all of it. Set up the shots
at every angle; run them online
24-7. Get beautiful stuff (like
scenery and greenery and style)
and get the ugliness (like cruelty
and quackery and rue). There's nothing
unastonishing – but get that, too. We have

to save it all, now that we can, and while.
Do close-ups with electron microscopes
and vaster pans with planetcams.
It may be getting close
to our last chance –
how many

millipedes or elephants are left?
How many minutes for mind-blinded men?
Use every lens you can – get Dubliners
in fisticuffs, the last Beijinger with
an abacus, the boy in Addis Ababa who feeds
the starving dog. And don't forget the cows

in neck-irons, when barns begin
to burn. The rollickers at clubs,
the frolickers at forage – take it all,
the space you need: it's curved. Let
mileage be footage, let years be light. Get
goggles for the hermitage, and shades for whorage.
Don't be boggled by totality: we're here to save the world

without exception. It will serve

as its own storage.

DODO'S CACA

It, too, is fossilized.
In time it has become
as valuable as he.
(In time, that is, there is

no waste – or all is waste,
to put it more depressingly.
Ah well, that takes the onus off
the opus. Lulled or gulled or

numbskulled, we
need not be suffered fools if all
is time's tomfoolery.)

~

The dream is by the drainage pipe.
The cheek is by the jowl.
All flesh to the inquiring eye,
the scavenging scatologist

gets the scoop from the shed.
But journalists (fair-weather friends!)
have been there first: the shed is full
of scoops befouled.

~

The present's sent
before its time. If time
has depth, you've got to dig
eternity – one, two! One, two! We're

on our way – each boy abed, each girl aglee,
each nobody aloft agrees we'll mark our meaning,
make our mark, the moment that the nowadays are done.
That's soon enough. That's presently. So shovel, little shovel-bird.

How far off could that be?

HACKERS CAN SIDEJACK COOKIES

a collage-homage to Guy L. Steele and Eric S. Raymond

A beige toaster is a maggotbox.
A bit bucket is a data sink.
Farkled is a synonym for hosed.
Flamage is a weenie problem.

A berserker wizard gets no score for treasure.
In MUDs one acknowledges
a bonk with an oif.
(There is a cosmic bonk/oif balance.)

Ooblick is play sludge.
A buttonhook is a hunchback.
Logic bombs can get inside
back doors. There were published bang paths
ten hops long. Designs succumbing
to creeping featuritis
are banana problems.
("I know how to spell banana,
but I don't know when to stop.")
Before you reconfigure,

mount a scratch monkey.
A dogcow makes
a moof. An aliasing bug
can smash the stack.

Who wrote these tunes,
these runes you need

black art to parse?
Don't think it's only

genius (flaming), humor (dry),
a briefcase of cerebral dust.
A hat's a shark fin, and the tilde's dash
is swung: the daughter of the programmer
has got her period. It's all about wetware at last,

and wetware lives in meatspace.

A BLIND

A blind of green
cedar, the branches cut just
at the changing of bands
(wood for wind, frond for trill,
logistics for lizard, scale for scale –

because the lineages
love Linnaeus, he's the
rex's lex), which leaves ourselves

an eyehole for the world,
after the weaving of one
over other and other
on one. Once it's built
it's a blind

sort of date. It's a nest with a mind
for a critter inside. And its charms
have a punch. And its hunches
have arms.

⁂

I saw it clearly then
at seven, in a Woolworth's floral aisle,
an aisle of plastic greenery, the moment that
the momentary struck me. There I stood
stock-still and swore

I'd never let it
leave my mind, I'd
nail it once and for all.
I grasped what I was

in the clutches of – a species
of unkindness, beating
at the brow. From then on,
then would have to be

forever known as now.

FAR NIENTE

Nothing is beyond our ken
And Everything is spurious.
Anything is close at hand
But we want Something – fast

And furious. Just to the stone men
Near the end of the fever
Takes the most curious
Almost forever. Nothing is farther

Again: Nothing is nearer
The truth. No one woke from the first –
We were wholly immersed –
Then we burst into Youth.

POSTCOCIOUS

Bubbling over at a glimpse
of yellow truck, singing out at every
dog or lollipop – a drop
of hat will do – hell, waking up
induces peals of laughter! They're abuzz
with businesses and glee. It's clear
to them what living's for.

It isn't clear to me.

For me each item's a line item,
each occasion an occasion for redress,
reclaiming, recompense, or rue. Given
time's best gift, I'm always
scheming to return it.
As for the language
of the love of life –

when did my soul unlearn it?

RECURRENT DREAM

Go, go, go, the daughter muttered
as the man (slo-mo) threw his plate at the wall
and the woman and children beside her
froze. She thought (and wrongly, as it all
turned out), I'll never grow
so furious at my
first mate.

No, no, no, the captain
(mom's new husband, feeling
hungry) admonished the daughter
when below the decks she turned
from the galley toward the head.
(For every impropriety she learned
new nouns. Much didn't match:
the stern, for example, so inviting,
and the bow so angry.)

Living rooms rolled by all night, and each one spilled
some golden cargo. Streets could not be told
from boundlessness, though now and then
their ends were nailed with metal letters.
Night would go on welling,
that was clear, until it got to flow, when
gently down the stream she'd aim

to row, row, row.

AGAPE

I could fly like a god –
went from zero to forty
and seven to five.
I could shift for myself,
michelining my time
round the workblocks and off-days.
Took a shine to my chassis and
took it uptown, where I saw in a highlight

the wreck it appeared – there it stopped
in a storefront, the shade of its shape
gave me pause – how it gaped – and then lo
from the O of its brain
stepped the creature itself –

just a day-numbered ape
with a clue it was clay.

STUDY UNDER FIRE

On one side only, even in the fog
The color seems conferred
By some sunset-nostalgic
Spray-paint specialist.

The color seems applied
On one side only, like
A love. Directional affection, from
The sun's southwest. With a quick

Reflexive tremor all will soon
Come down to air and bare bone –
Clean of vanity and veil. Meanwhile,
Believing that the tree gives rise

To all this fire, we feel
Excited in its zone, conceive
The shines to be requited, and begin
To love a little nature of our own.

ON PURPOSE LAID

Bitten hind- and forequarters by Jove
I beat a blind retreat from love.

But he's there, too. I've seen his gray-
blue fingerprints on every

wrinkle of the brain. That's why I grew
so skeptic of a heavenly escape.

You build a craft, you have
to man it. (Juno cannot help me:

jealous of all animals that ever
got off on a planet.)

GRANNY'S SONG

If the fact itself were not
at odds with most of my hopes
for human life, I'd want

to know why sex was always best
when I stood to lose the most.
Why make its charms so devilishly

proximal to risk?
The patterns ought to favor
children's best protection – not

one parent hardened and one hurt;
one predator, one weak. But nurturance
appeared to have no part

in our old fastest appetites – our grappling hooks
and eye-meats. Well, a mortally afflicted tree
will scatter seed. That's nature's way

of furthering its kind. In my own
sixties (here where issue's not the issue –
not unless I go to Delhi for

an embryo implant, and let me tell you
I am not *that* nuts) – here newly
sixtified, I say, I'd settle for

a kindness: tender looks not
tenterhooks; a cuddle,
not a cattle-prod. Dear god,

you made me pull away from every
club and strut and hoe. Don't now
on my account, sweet chariot,

swing so damn low.

ABOUT THE HEAD

In the old days it was all
phrenologists and mentalists,
feelers for speed bumps.

Several rubbers later there was lunch,
and the diamonded mind
and the spaded heart
were equally sedated,

and the club,
the club in whose name
so much was done, the club that could trace
its roots back to an ash tree,
and its branches up
to an ash cloud,

the club that let in and that disallowed
the thought of so many –
ingeniously giving members
bullhorns for our little voices,
leather for our liabilities of skin –
the products of its expertises hooking
dugs to suction-cups
and penises to clever
lover-tubes, docilities
to stanchions – keeping the consumer
from those messy overflows – oh yes,

the clickogenic club – it's now on its way
out, going the slope of the oil- and

cowmen, under a wave of nouveau
spunk, as reproduction comes
in plastic, tungsten,
dazzleworks of circuitry – no
boring boards! The club with all its antique
codes and codicils will have to

club itself out, out of courtesy, on the path
to a virtually productive heaven – let the gentlemen
agree. Their sons, the slackers with the liquor, hand it on
to generation Z, that need not multiply or sleep. The stock
of alphabets runs out, the line of swollen lifetimes hits
the point of several seconds flat, and any smidgen
beats a bludgeon. Just a blip behind the eyes

works better than a bruiser with a bat.

UNTO HIGH HEAVEN

Most people trust in will
and dream of power.
The man of the moment would kill
to be Man of the Hour.

Most people live by asking
daylight's worth.
My God, they're multitasking
everywhere on Earth.

But to inherit it –
my Liege! – don't stoop
to seek. Pass up the privilege
of being meek.

I CANNOT CLEAR MY EYES

On his chain in the merciless sun
is a dog; on macadam a run-over cat –

and what's that moving mud
near the murder of wheels? How can

these crow-crowds bear their kind? The victim
screeches in the flap but can't outfly them:

luckless, maybe sick... A relative of ours.
It's not that we lack luck or luster, family

or sleep. But here at god's own
Earth Day barbecue we are

the blackest sheep.

PHILOSOPHER ORDERS CRISPY PORK

I love him so, this animal I pray
was treated kindly. Let me pay as much as even
greater pig-lovers see fit

to guarantee him that. As for his fat,
I'd give up years yes years of my
own life for such

a gulpable semblable.
(My life! Such as it is, this
liberality of leaves! The world

won't need those seventeen more
poems, after all, there being
so few subjects to be treated. Three

if by subject we mean anyone
submitted to another's will. Two
if by subject we mean

topic. One if by death we wind up
meaning love. And none
if a subject must entail

the curlicue's indulgence of itself.)

THOUS BY THE THOUSANDS

There's too much gobbling
going on. Gobble up the baby
with his cheeks! Gobble up the girlhood,
with its eyes. Gobble up the novel with its world
and scoop the lovers up, to coop them in.
After the gulletful, the lip
is dabbed. No trouble.

Just a single gob can multiply
into a gobble's worth – or one small rub
into a rubbled history – the hag a whole
damned marketplace. And one scribe's
nib? Well, after all, you get
the point. Get out the bib
(and lengthen up the eye).

Take that – a double-handled cup! Take
this – a clamor for acclaim. Throw in
a fiddle for Fidelio, and for the little lady

baby Bob, a nodding ornament.

The gleam of insight dimmed into a glimmer.
Our awe before a one-and-only
bogged down into frequentatives. From the break

in space and time – a crack across the priceless pottery –
we crackled up production lines. The thunderbolt to shake

your being's very frame – the heavens' way
of sparking up a conversation – that

got channeled down into white noise.
We slept in letters, woke in stitches,
toggled off and on. At last, forever

happened: we appeared in Oz, on Death TV,
where the illusions of expanded view
could not diminish anybody's hunger.
Given an allowance, we began
to spend eternity, all but agog

in our designer goggles.

ILL-MADE ALMIGHTY

No man has more assurance than a bad poet.

MARTIAL

The Logos thrives, it is crawling
with bugs. The lecturcrs arc tccming –

memorific, futurized, dead-certain they'll go
unsurprised. They don't know nows

as we do, true to no clear
destination. (We can't even

act our age: it's over-understudied.) Steady
as you go. The greatest waves are barely

bearable, alive's ill-
read already,

and the Skipper is sick
of the terrible lit

graffiti in the head...

AND THE GREATEST OF THESE

Stupidity's no grounds for our despair.
It drives or drowses everywhere –
waxen, bristling, pitted, slick –
as variously textured as
notoriously tough. It ought
arouse more wonder than aversion:
cases most complex are hexed, and know it,
while the simplest merely grin into the void.
A sort of wisdom, either way, this
being short on wit.

Nor may despair accrue
to humankind's unsightliness – the humped one no one loves,
the scrawny and the scrofulous, the pimpled and the pocked –
who hasn't lost all sight of beauty,
once the beauty talked?

I can't lose hope over the way
we tort as we retort, reveal as we redress –
I can't regret the spank of life, its sparkling
more-or-less. Where heartlands lie the lowest
(stream and meadow, desert, swamp)
I trample on, I keep up hope
at every everloving turn.
Each turn, that is, except

the wickedest: when cruelty
comes cackling from its
crackhouses in nature – hell
must help me then because
I lose all heart at hurt intended. Not just

humans, after all, who massacre
their cousins and their dogs. You'll see
the crows gang up as well, with bloody beaks and
malice and intent, bedeviling some half-defeathered
brother to his death; or, dashing out the kitchen door,
the pampered shepherds lunging from
the farm-wife's kibbled kiss, and just for this:

to fang the haunches of a fawn – not once
but seven times (it seems inexpertise is all the more
excited by the sufferer)... The heart

must bear it all, apparently, or burn, or dim, as
claw on claw the creatures in the tank
go scrambling to outclimb the creature crush.
On days like that, when cruelty is king,
and sun in swill appears to swim, I thank
no lucky stars for life: It wants to take a lover

limb from limb.

FOR WANT OF BETTER WORDS

You lose your
grip, you could say.
That handy bag.

The ones you poured your life into
were ripped away – their treasured senses,
knacks of narrative,

abruptly stopped
with mud.
So you get number –

adjective that never should have been

susceptible of the comparative.

~

You are not faithful, hopeful, kind –
are those the three? (The only three? so many?)
Must the one be greater, as the Scriptures say?

The buck cannot stop anywhere. Once gotten out of hand,
it goes on growing in the mind. In masterworks of map

the big fishfinders
sweep the seeing globe –
with people always
coming out on top. One man

professes to believe
no hope exists where there's
no love: he opens up

a sex-toy shop.

~

Above it all, behind it all, beyond
its all-or-nothingness, the only
opening that counts –

a countlessness the stars have stood for
even as their senses moved –

an opening the measurers adore
because it marks the end of ends. And mind
is mesmerized by such unfathomable states, past all
high fives, deep sixes, and the wondrous
horizontal eight – a nowhere

faster than the newsflash,
faster than the speeding hearse.
You're late in your
one-upmanship,
your craft, your

universe...

SPACE BAR

Lined up behind the space bartender
is the meaning of it all, the vessels
marked with letters, numbers,
signs. Beyond the flats

the monitor looms, for all the world
like the world: images and
motions, weeping women,
men in hats. I have killed

many happy hours here,
with my bare hands, as TV
passes for IV, among
the space cadets and dingbats.

MYRRHA TO THE SOURCE

O fluent one, O muscle full of hydrogen,
O stuff of grief, whom the Greeks
accuse of spoiling souls,

whose destiny is downward,
whose reflecting's up – I think
I must have come from you.

Just one more cup.

WITH THE MOON

March 26, 2007

Utterly impossible for a person of some
(how you say?) *literary discretion*

to attack the blossoming
goddamn cherry trees –
and by attack I mean attach
her ever overly-involving
meathooks of admiring to them (mire and ad being alike
inherently besmirching). He would never

love me, for example; that was only
a commercial break, while I was putting in
a lifetime. Nature loves its laws
above its instances. But Mrs. Christ
I wasn't born to be. (The dogwood made
too many bloody claims on its Virginias.
In its stranglehold of jurisdictions there was no
West Hag or Northern Hussydale for me
to hurry home to.) Moving,
moved, without avail, by doubt,
and wary of a human's fondest hopes,
I noticed that the slope was littered
with the optimists. But as I lived I wasn't quite alone

in misbegetting love and mis-conceiving laws.
Addictable to goods, one still admires the good
while, full of will, we wheel upon
a planetary whim, no more than

incidentals in a sunscape: gravity-employees,
tissue-issuers, and slaves of rhythm. It is utterly

impossible to say

how (charged unto combustibility) the cherry petals
are not just a dummy's decoration – something to forget
ourselves in, paparazzi-flashes or perfumeries
of pink. A jilter and a jiltee aren't distinct
inside the litter's heap: their mothers indiscriminately lick
the little nodes and navels. No, he wouldn't ever

love me, in so many words. He'd maybe lay
a hand on me, asleep.

THE SONG OF SKEPTOMAI LOU

Old wives, I wish I could
be one of you. Instead
I am the born old maid.

Old maid emeritus,
let's say – the squid
whose erudition hugs
too many clams at once –
heart full of ink. With my
verdichter's digits, I could practice

having crushes. But appetites for permanence

went whirring on. So did the ring
of close calls (all collect). Even the elders
wrecked their roadsters, just to have one
date with the tow truck. Drivers loved
their doctors into deep intensive care – ah, why
go there – old wives! I did remain intact,

was checked, rechecked, racked up, A-plus –
that's better than perfect, right? That much,
let's say, is understood. (I'm speaking
Old Grammarian, you'll recognize,
where something understood

is something missing.)

MISSING MEANING

The mystery of speaking every day
So plainly from a face she cannot see

Unsettles her unless she can forget
The things she knows and sink back into

What she means. (Her times
Seem overfocused

On the frame – wire-rimmed or
Tortoiseshell – and nothing

Taken at face value. The skeptic
Backs his watch, watches his back,

That much is given.) But
The View-Master's skewed

By a hairbreadth or eyebridge:
There goes heaven.

GOOD OLD GOD

He's a hoot, with his flips of the nickel,
his penchant for law, and his playing with volts –

let the lovers be struck! (It's his joke, on our dime.) And by Jove
what a backside he turns! And by gum what bedeviled
expressions! A scowl full of thous, and the gene pool
is shot. "Thou shalt flower for moments – and rot

for the rest – being flesh, being given to
lust. Say you wanted an ocean of
feeling, or time? Here's a puddle to
come from, a crack and a crotch." He's a hoot,

don't you think? – there above the commotion, just
finding the bright side, just
winding his watch...

HALF BORDER AND HALF LAB

⁂

Customs and chemistry
made a name for themselves
and it was Spot. He's gone to some
ou-topos now, the dirty dog, doctor of
crotches, digger of holes. Your airy
clarities be damned, he loved our must
and even our mistakes – why hit him, then,
who did us good? He's dead, who ought
to be at home. He's damned
put out; and so am I.

⁂

When blue is carried through, the law is red.
When noon is said and done, it's dusk again.
The greed for table makes the greed for bed.
So *cave canem,* even stars have litters – little
lookers, cacklers, killers... Morning raises up
the hackled men. (Among our ilk, what's milk
but opportunity for spillers?)

⁂

He saved our sorry
highfalutin souls – the heavens haven't
saved a fly. Orion's canniness who can
condone? – that starring story, strapping blade! –
and Sirius is just a Fido joke. No laughter shakes
the firmament. But O

the family dog, the Buddha-dog – son
of a bitch! *he* had
a funny bone –

DOMESTIQUE

Surfaces to scrape or wipe,
a screwdriver to be applied
to slime-encrusted soles, the spattered

hallways, wadded bedding – and
in quantities astounding (in the corners,
under furniture, behind the curtains)

fluff and dander spread by curs
the breeder called nonshedding...
It's a dog's life I myself must lead,

day in, day out – with never a Sunday edition –
while they lie around on their couches like poets,
and study the human condition.

GLASS HOUSE

Everything obeyed our laws and
we just went on self-improving
till a window gave us pause and
there the outside world was, moving.

Five apartment blocks swept by,
the trees and ironwork and headstones
of the next town's cemetery.
Auto lots. Golf courses. Rest homes.
Blue-green fields and perishable vistas
wars had underscored in red
were sweeping past,
with cloudscapes, just

as if the living room were dead.
Which way to look? Nonnegative?
Nonplussed? (Unkilled? Unkissed?)
Look out, you said; the sight's on us:

If we don't move, we can't be missed.

FROM THE TOWER

Insanity is not a want of reason.
It is reason's overgrowth, a calculating kudzu.
Explaining why, in two-ton manifesti, thinkers sally forth
with testaments and pipe bombs. Heaven help us:

spare us all your meaningful designs. Shine
down or shower forth, but for our earthling sakes
ignore all prayers followed by *against,* or *for.*
Teach us to bear life's senselessness, and our

own insignificance. Let's call that sanity.
The terrifying prospect isn't some poor
sucker in a La-Z-Boy, inclined to jokes,
remotes, or sweets. It is the busy hermeneut,

so serious he's sour, intent on making
meaning of us all –

and bursting from the tower to the streets.

MAN IN THE STREET

He claps a hand
Across the gaping hole –

Or else the sight
Might well inside to

Melt the mind – if any
Thinking spoke

Were in the wheel,
Or any real

Fright-fragments broke
Out of the gorge to

Soak the breast, the meaning might
Incite a stroke. Best

Press against it, close
The clawhole, stand

In stupor, petrified. The dream
Be damned, the deeps defied.

(The hand's to keep
The scream inside.)

MARY'S REMINDER

An oddity of war
(among the many) is:
it has to educate attackers

in the ones attacked, incurring, as war does,
some counterswells abroad and then at home –
two sides on every side. Our young

are learning Arabic, and wrapping up
their heads: hair-trigger in a Supercut.
We're struck and then

instructed by our strife: the shades
of difference between eleven, say, and twelve –
trousers and trusses, toys and knives,

a handshake and a landmine.
God, you were a boy
for all your life.

CREATURE CRUSH

I

Dear God, if you ever were
(and I have to go on being) alive,
at least don't make me have to see
(forever in my mind as now on my TV)
the likes of this poor

furred familiar, hauled by neckchain
to be eyeballed there in the public square in Kathmandu –

this miserable monkey, made alert
with a yank toward the knife of his keeper.
Riveted, misgiving, every morning he is made
to cry – nicked at the neck, so onlookers will register

how sharp the situation is. But that's just foreplay,
because then the knife-arm does (what must inform his nightmares
endlessly while other monkeys sleep) the drama of a three-foot thrust

directly at the creature's gut – so he recoils, of course,
and has to freeze in that unthinkable contortion (neck hauled close
to his tormentor's gaze). They stay like that for an eternity. A minute,

more or less.

II

The monkey's quivering. Today his quick responses mean
he'll live to do another show. (Someday, like every
other animal, he's going

to be sick, or sore, or slow –
no sweat. Another monkey can be got
with coins this monkey's agony has bought.)

III

The people crane to see,
not necessarily because they're cruel – I hope
they're horrified – they do avert their gazes, now
and then, but cannot keep
from gawking once again. Myself,
I wince from here. I am as apt to stare

as any of my fellow men.

IV

Eventually the monkey is required
to walk among the humans,
pass a hat. Those who have cried
give extra. (What's the worse

perverseness of this plan,
the helplessness or the complicity?)
Apparently I neither can

release the monkey
nor assassinate the man.

NOCEBO

Rather than this,
I would gladly feel nothing.
Give me some more

anesthetic thing.
My zoom control is set,
it seems, on oversmall: all Hamlets
and gloomlets. It's a sin to hold

unhappiness so dear, or dearness
to a price, I know. Well-being ought
to counterbalance misery, in all the universe's
mass. By Heraclitus and by God, across
the range of states, the contraries should
balance out, so suffering and satisfaction mark
a single spectrum's sore extremities. (The mind's
designed, declared De Vries, to keep the ears
from grating on each other.) Oh but you, you

screw the balance up, you human animal:
of names the only caller and dropper, making
scapegoats out of badgers, snakes, and grouse –
they're answering for *you*. And where's my fabled
freedom, if I cannot liberate

the creatures of my word, the eye
of my TV, the wiring of my house? What sense
might the excruciated make, whose ravenous receptors
(over veldts of happy elephants)

flock to the one shocked mouse?

DARK VIEW

The sun that puts its spokes in every
Wheel of manhandle and tree

Derives its path of seashines
(Spiritual centrality) from my

Regard. I sent it
My regards. Some yards

Of lumen from the fabrika
Have come unbolted in the likes

Of it, or maybe
In the likes of me – a long

Unweaving or recarding I
Cannot recall begun – and there

Before my eyes the palm
Puts lashes round the sun.

TREE FARM

Tempted by restive night to make
a festive figure, given each
an ax and hour there,
an hour before the evening
news, the human beings flock to this

still-living stand of minded pine.
The shapes are perfect
triangles. The range
has been arranged to hide the wild.
(But every old saw has a human child.)

The little trees are planted from
the blacktop to the fence. They can't
escape the blinking Santas or
the hundred Rudolphs
on the looping tape...

Manned by some unsteady creature,
one Dodge truck has backed into the crèche;
and thanks to pigeons, several wise men are defiled.
A city father and his son, who had
to sit all day, have come

from officework and school; they know the ways
of pencil sharpeners: they press against their tools.
Alas, the saw is dull, or bent; they dent the tree,
they pull; it must submit. They drag it off
against its grain, and up the stairs

toward a gaping living room. There is the table,
with its tethered bird. There is the woodstove where
Thanksgiving's trees were burned. The evergreen has got
its hackles up, as otherwise it couldn't mean to –
spreads its arms across the jamb, and will and will

and will not budge. That's how a little grudge
can shake enormous premises: one minute
you are celebrating, and the next –
your Christmas a catastrophe,
your condo just a lean-to.

WHICH IS GIVEN FOR YOU

A carnation the crux
of the matter, heart

close-read. The head
not only minded: minding.

Participles hot, thoughts in-
sufficiently wooden: flow

in the flesh. See notes
on hand (the human being

moving). Feelings aflutter:
falls afoot: all healing

failed, all hanging fought.
They nailed him and

they nailed him good.

THE RIVER OVERFLOWS THE RIFT

From every reach of field to come
to gather in a clump, stock-still,
as rain begins to fall to fill
the hole where he is being
lowered, lovers

are allotted
two feet each, whereon to stand,
withstand, or just stand by

the place he's placed,
here in the woods,
in the world, in the
moon-rid solar system.
Humans do seem dim.

But later little lights will rise,
to float on something we can't see,
and pinpoints may be

angels. (Or else hell has fireflies.)

~

Before a human face
a glance could light without
alighting, gleams meander through
the untagged trees, a stream into the pattern
lend its thread. But then we came affixing
barbs and snags, and until all of us

are done away, a million lilies will be stilled
by some arranger's hands, a billion stones
be hauled and heaped by heart, to stand
for words, where words aren't going
to be kept. The word

must move: the minute does.
Its starred expanses dazzle
humankind (wherever there's a mind
for wonderment). In time

the glimmers of the uncontained
outcourse even a lover's frozen frown,
the silver wave revives the mower. Glowers
by glow are overcome, flowers by flow.

THE GIFT

From underwater you can't see
a thing above: a sun, or a cloud,
or a man in a boat. You see
the bottom of the boat.

And everywhere below it –
flocks of glitter, brilliantly
communicating schools.
You see the calm
translucencies in groves, a sway
of peaceful flags. Above is silver
impassivity – reflective lid.
So why look out?
No out exists.

The sky, each time it's wounded,
heals at once. A zippering across it
instantly dissolves. A wet suit's foot
or a long black line behind a plummet,
or the sudden angling boomerang
(murre in a hurry to
zigzag down) all come
as pure surprises, passing thoughts

that leave no afterimage.

~

But we have lived above it all instead,
our feet on the ground, our heads

in the clouds, where there's
no ceiling sealing us from heaven.

Drawn into every storybook of stars – the spark-lit
universes, countlessness of dust – we think along
those phosphorescent ways there must (the brain
lights up a schoolroom rule) live others
like ourselves – in worlds
as mirror-mesmerized.

As mine, let's say, or hers. And so it was
around the fifty-seventh month
of her life's underlife (a mindless blind
metastasis of cells) we sent each other

messages by e-mail, sudden, simultaneous,
because of dreams. In hers, the ancestors
were waiting, just across a lake, but she
found no equipment in her
circumstances of canoe.
The paddle on the water
drifted far and
farther off.
She saw it

touch my boat, she said.
She saw me shove it back, across the surface,
safely to her hand, so she could get
where she'd be found.
Dear god, give me
a faith like that.

In my dream we both drowned.

NOT TO BE DWELLED ON

Self-interest cropped up even there,
the day I hoisted three, instead
of the ceremonially called-for two,
spadefuls of loam on top
of the coffin of my friend.

Why shovel more than anybody else?
What did I think I'd prove? More love
(mud in her eye)? More will to work?
(Her father what, a shirker?) Christ,
what wouldn't anybody give
to get that gesture back?

She cannot die again; and I
do nothing but re-live.

PRACTICE PRACTICE PRACTICE

I know it's unseemly
to keep on grieving, go on
sorrowing this way.
It's a presumption, some might say
(since everybody loses someone,
why should anybody claim
to bear them all, all
over, all at once,
each day?).

Unseemly to obsess
on suffering, in such
milieus, the top five
tourist destinations full

of dogs in hot cars, birds abandoned,
toddlers come to understand they can't
be coddled from now on, and grown men,
lovelorn, throwing up in bushes near the dance...
(Even the King is lonely: the *Enquirer*'s lucre
has seduced the page. Alas, he loved

that bobbed, that bobbing
head.) And in the under-
funded hospice, there's an only
irritable night-nurse. In a home with a
capital H, in daily and unfettered joys
an idiot appears advanced. We wish
we could, ourselves, slow down. Instead

we get on with the show. Rehearse
means Quick now, bring those big

black limos back around.

BOTH SIDES SNIPE AT THE HOLY GHOST

Jesus with a joke rifle. Cockiness before
the cannonade. Do we feel
better after? Feel
which way?

Are we not
hard of hearing, who discharge
so many rounds of laughter?

Are we not ridden with it – riddled with it –
friendly fire? Thank God we doze
a couple hundred hours a month
and dozens of those hours

add up to make a better
balanced life. (The all-or-nothings
kill you after all – the shooter and the shot
are kissing cousins. Respire, expire.
You learn more than you earn. The only
old gold is regret.) Instead,

let's lure the nestlings back, what do you say?
Not blast each second thing to smithereens.
Otherwise, active or passive, wired
or winging ("live" or live) something
escapes us – tertium quid, rarest of birds:

our buckshot evanescence.
There it is! – in every fray

of oppositions, singing thirds.

NO SEX FOR PRIESTS

The horse in harness suffers:
he's not feeling up to snuff.

The feeler's sensate but the cook
pronounces lobsters tough.

The chain's too short: the dog's at pains
to reach a sheaf of shade. One half a squirrel's

whirling there, upon the interstate.
That ruff around the monkey's eye

is cancer. Only god's impervious:
he's deaf and blind. But he's not dumb:

to answer for it all, his spokesmen
aren't allowed to come.

caelum bibere [drink some sky]

LUCILIUS

BOONDOCKS

We come from there – that
clattering tautology. The boon's

the boom – what lowers a load
from the tottering sky;

the dock's the planks and pilings,
strictness of the structures made

so we can walk on water, put
these franking footholds on

the riled-up rookery; the dock's
the bracing that the boat is lashed to:

tarry trunk, and tacky creosote.
An orange star attaches to a moment,

waves toward a slo-mo lobe.
A finger's inch outruns

a yardarm's reach – the boon's
the rope, the slip, the pilings, and

the sound. We come from there,
and we want more. Another ton

of sky-stuff winches down.

NOTHING IS TOO SMALL

We have turned,
we can't help it,
the sheer horror of it
to a story we can put
in a hip pocket, put

behind us, let us say,
so we don't have to
suffer ceaselessly.

But the soul requires
some toll of the eternal
to be taken. There are traces
of the heightened feeling here
and there: a whole year later
someone can't forget

how one of her feet was naked –
and the threshold where her temple rested
should have been swept better. Even five years

haven't taken out of someone's eye
what showed up in the streaming
whirlpools to one side
of that particular
TV (the second plane was

plowing through its high-rise): there
a speckled harbor seal
had raised his head up

out of the current's fastest flow, and
stayed the longest time,
just looking all around.

As if amazed at how things stand.

Or maybe how they go.

MOVING WALKWAY

I would have stood for memories
if memories would will it.
Memories would not. They flew
from every stronghold

and immediacy staked its claims –
in featherdusting wind, in watercolored name,
in waves of genotype. Ungovernable
polymorph, the flow was disinclined

to be revised, or be reduced – could not be boxed,
could not be kept, for carrying to other
spots in time (posterities to go, or
merriments to come). One step and we

went meters; seven more, and we became
pure haste: fastheaded, leaving all
steadfastnesses behind, all tendencies
of centuries toward

the halted hallways, marble men.

THANKS FOR THAT LAST HEARTTHROB

Little being moved,
at last, give thanks.

One doesn't want
always to be bound
to change.

And whether by weathers
(the ins and outs of them)
or by bloody bulldozer
(who lullabied that baby?) –

whether by nature's nature
or your own (O man, you draw
a fine damn line!) – it hurts to be

at a mercy, or a wit's end. (Few believe
the wit's end hurts – or any part of it, for that
sad matter. Utter folly, once
such errors have begun,

the big being moved
most of all, after all,

by the littlest one.)

LEAF-LITTER ON ROCK FACE

Things are not
unmoving (or else what

is inging for?). These things
once-living

drift toward the stone
more movingly for any human glance

that passes over them. The wind
wells up to spill a trail

of onces off the nevers,
take opaqueness from an eye

to mind, or near it.
Every rocking

takes some leaving
to a stonish spirit.

WHO NEEDS IT

~

If language could be trusted to be true,
the hardest would be loudest,
softest, soft. But think again: the joke's
on you. Against a granite face the sea

has knocked for years without
much fuss or brouhaha –
just here and there a little
cracking sound, a suck
in a pocket of cranny.
But give it a load of beach-flesh – and

you'll never hear the end of it: the pumps in full
palaver with the valvers, every grain
resounding, every pound. You'd think
slap-happy waves might hush, at such

soft-sanded touches. On the contrary there is
a cardiac clamor, a sumptuousness,
roaring into space. The ocean's noisiest

around the giving place.

~

O stranded earth, O beach of
fellow men, I see you selve and cleave in every
single way you can. And all the ways add up:

each needleworker's couch and bounded town,
each humming humanific lobe has thrown
its tune into the planetary wave. But what's

the message of our massing,
past these minuscules of parts? Is it a song of manyness,
or tininess? This suburb-reverb spilling out,
gregarious, egregious, from the globe –
does it go on for light-years, and convulse

the quietudes of heaven? Wake
some star-shells? Stir some dulse?
My guess is yes, since endlessness

needs us to take its pulse.

MOURNER'S KADDISH

Let's make it
bigger and more awesome,
god's big name in the world,
the world he made as only
lonely gods would do. (And may he make
a better one, by god, before he's through.)

May his big name go out beyond
all space and time, the way a heart goes out.
Be "hallowed and honored, extolled and exalted,
adored and acclaimed" – to use the big old words
(though human hymns can't fathom him, nor get
an inkling of his eye). May he make peace

despite our spite, and may our heavy spirits fly.
May he who writes the music soon arrange
to make the meaning clear – if not today
then (let us pray)

before the last musicians die.

THE MICROSCOPE

Through petri dishes' rings
life is transmogrified. When we
look into things, we see

there's space inside.

MEDIUM AS METEOROLOGIST

Listening in or looking out,
alert to othernesses, grasping something
now and then, a hand or pattern,
circle, sympathy, or symbol (one side trembles
when the other one grows hot) – not

knowing one is feeling, past
five-minded touch, one wants to feel
secure. What comes is no more than
an airwave, lick of love, or lack
of candlepower. Focus on the glimmer

as the blown rain batters us broadside
from the haunts of nature, just beyond
the blinds. Our knowing is a feel
for the nuance: our sentience itself
the whole séance.

AN UNDERWORLDLINESS

for Aileen Winter Mostel

Maybe a maker makes
another out – by the mark
of the mechanism – keyboard cabaret –
clown in love with his own club (one foot's
spondee). I turned it over

in my sleeping head, that
fallow feeling – pillow a numbset's
handskull – till from fidgeting synapses

rose an REM of ultivated answer –
all-but-seeing

eye on a stem – the glancer born to blow
by way of aneurysm... (at what
altitude or depth, what
certitude or asterisk,
nobody seeing
could see through).
The star was visibly

newfangled, brimming over from
the wave or cup one was

to drain or fill – who knew? No
thinking would contain it now.

Sidewise it angled, and shone up.

ABOUT THE AUTHOR

Heather McHugh is the author of thirteen books of poetry, translation, and literary essays, including a Griffin International Poetry Prize translation, as well as Pulitzer and National Book Award finalist volumes. McHugh has taught literature and writing for over three decades, most regularly at the University of Washington in Seattle and in the low-residency M.F.A. Program for Writers at Warren Wilson College. From 1999 to 2005 she served as a chancellor of the Academy of American Poets, and in 2000 she was elected a fellow of the American Academy of Arts and Sciences.

Lannan Literary Selections

For two decades Lannan Foundation has supported the publication and distribution of exceptional literary works. Copper Canyon Press gratefully acknowledges their support.

LANNAN LITERARY SELECTIONS 2009

Michael Dickman, *The End of the West*

James Galvin, *As Is*

Heather McHugh, *Upgraded to Serious*

Lucia Perillo, *Inseminating the Elephant*

Connie Wanek, *On Speaking Terms*

RECENT LANNAN LITERARY SELECTIONS FROM COPPER CANYON PRESS

Lars Gustafsson, *A Time in Xanadu,* translated by John Irons

David Huerta, *Before Saying Any of the Great Words: Selected Poems,* translated by Mark Schafer

June Jordan, *Directed by Desire: The Collected Poems*

Sarah Lindsay, *Twigs and Knucklebones*

W.S. Merwin, *Migration: New & Selected Poems*

Valzhyna Mort, *Factory of Tears,* translated by Franz Wright and Elizabeth Oehlkers Wright

Taha Muhammad Ali, *So What: New & Selected Poems, 1971–2005,* translated by Peter Cole, Yahya Hijazi, and Gabriel Levin

Dennis O'Driscoll, *Reality Check*

Kenneth Rexroth, *The Complete Poems of Kenneth Rexroth*

Ruth Stone, *In the Next Galaxy*

C.D. Wright, *One Big Self: An Investigation*

Matthew Zapruder, *The Pajamaist*

For a complete list of Lannan Literary Selections from Copper Canyon Press, please visit Partners on our Web site: www.coppercanyonpress.org

The Chinese character for poetry is made up of two parts: "word" and "temple." It also serves as pressmark for Copper Canyon Press.

Since 1972, Copper Canyon Press has fostered the work of emerging, established, and world-renowned poets for an expanding audience. The Press thrives with the generous patronage of readers, writers, booksellers, librarians, teachers, students, and funders—everyone who shares the belief that poetry is vital to language and living.

Major funding has been provided by:

Anonymous

Beroz Ferrell & The Point, LLC

Cynthia Hartwig and Tom Booster

Lannan Foundation

Lannan

National Endowment for the Arts

NATIONAL
ENDOWMENT
FOR THE ARTS

Cynthia Lovelace Sears and Frank Buxton

Washington State Arts Commission

For information and catalogs:

COPPER CANYON PRESS
Post Office Box 271
Port Townsend, Washington 98368
360-385-4925
www.coppercanyonpress.org

The interior is set in ITC Bodoni Twelve Book. ITC Bodoni was designed by Sumner Stone, Jim Parkinson, Holly Goldsmith, and Janice Fishman in 1994 after research into Bodoni's original steel punches. Book design by Valerie Brewster, Scribe Typography. Printed on archival-quality paper at McNaughton & Gunn, Inc.